FEMINIZATION

EXPLANATIONS TO ALL THE CONCEPTS OF FEMINIZATION

DR. LELAND BURTON

Table of Contents

CHAPTER ONE

INTRODUCTION

Feminizing hormone treatment normally is utilized by transgender ladies and nonbinary humans to deliver physical changes within the frame which can be on account of female hormones within the route of puberty. Those adjustments are known as secondary sex traits. This hormone remedy allows better align the frame with someone's gender identification. Feminizing hormone remedy is also referred to as gender-declaring hormone remedy.

Feminizing hormone therapy includes taking remedy to block the movement of the hormone testosterone. It also includes taking the hormone estrogen. Estrogen lowers the quantity of testosterone the frame makes. It also triggers the improvement of feminine secondary intercourse developments. Feminizing hormone therapy may be achieved on my own or collectively with feminizing surgical procedure.

Now not all people chooses to have feminizing hormone remedy. It is able to affect fertility and sexual feature, and it might cause health issues. Communicate in conjunction with your health care issuer approximately the risks and blessings for you.

Feminizing hormone treatment is used to change the frame's hormone stages. Those hormone adjustments motive physical adjustments that help higher align the body with a person's gender identity.

In some times, human beings searching for feminizing hormone remedy experience pain or misery due to the fact their gender identity differs from their intercourse assigned at begin or from their intercourse-associated bodily tendencies. This condition is known as gender dysphoria.

Feminizing hormone remedy can:

Enhance psychological and social properly-being.

Ease psychological and emotional distress associated with gender.

Decorate pleasure with sex.

Beautify super of lifestyles.

Your fitness care organization would probable recommend in competition to feminizing hormone therapy in case you:

Have a hormone-touchy most cancers, along with prostate most cancers.

Have issues with blood clots, consisting of whilst a blood clot paperwork in a deep vein, a circumstance known as deep vein thrombosis, or a there is a blockage in one of the pulmonary arteries of the lungs, called a pulmonary embolism.

Have large medical conditions which have

now not been addressed.

Have behavioral health conditions that have now not been addressed.

Have a situation that limits your potential to offer your knowledgeable consent.

Risks

Studies has observed that feminizing hormone therapy can be secure and powerful while delivered through a fitness care agency with know-how in transgender care. Talk to your health care company approximately questions or concerns you've got concerning the modifications for you to take location in your frame because of feminizing hormone remedy.

Complications can encompass:

Blood clots in a deep vein or in the lungs

Heart problems

Immoderate tiers of triglycerides, a form of fats, within the blood

High tiers of potassium inside the blood

High stages of the hormone prolactin inside the blood

Nipple discharge

Weight advantage

Infertility

Immoderate blood pressure

Kind 2 diabetes

Stroke

Proof suggests that those who take feminizing hormone therapy may additionally have an elevated chance of breast maximum cancers whilst in comparison to cisgender men — men whose gender identity aligns with societal norms associated with their sex assigned at transport. However the chance is not more than that of cisgender ladies.

To lessen chance, the intention for people taking feminizing hormone remedy is to maintain hormone ranges in the range it honestly is common for cisgender women.

Fertility

Feminizing hormone treatment may restriction your fertility. If possible, it's miles quality to make selections approximately fertility earlier than starting remedy. The risk of eternal infertility will increase with lengthy-term use of hormones. That is specifically actual for individuals who begin hormone therapy earlier than puberty starts offevolved offevolved. Even after stopping hormone remedy, your testicles may not get better sufficient to make sure thought with out infertility treatment.

If you want to have natural kids, communicate for your health care agency approximately freezing your sperm in advance than you begin feminizing hormone treatment. That gadget is called sperm cryopreservation.

The way you prepare

Earlier than you begin feminizing hormone therapy, your health care provider assesses your fitness. This facilitates address any scientific conditions that would have an effect to your treatment. The evaluation can also moreover encompass:

A review of your personal and circle of relatives scientific history.

A physical examination.

Lab exams.

A assessment of your vaccinations.

Screening assessments for a few situations and illnesses.

Identity and control, if wished, of tobacco

use, drug use, alcohol use illness, HIV or exceptional sexually transmitted infections.

Speak approximately sperm freezing and fertility.

You moreover can also would in all likelihood have a behavioral fitness assessment by manner of a business enterprise with expertise in transgender health. The assessment might also confirm:

Gender identity.

Gender dysphoria.

Mental fitness issues.

Sexual health worries.

The effect of gender identification at work, at faculty, at domestic and in social settings.

Risky behaviors, including substance use or use of unapproved silicone injections, hormone treatment or dietary supplements.

Assist from circle of relatives, pals and caregivers.

Your dreams and expectancies of treatment.

Care planning and observe-up care.

Human beings younger than age 18, along side a determine or mum or dad, should see a hospital treatment company and a behavioral fitness company with knowledge in pediatric transgender fitness to talk about the dangers and benefits of hormone treatment and gender transitioning in that age company.

CHAPTER TWO

What you may anticipate

You need to start feminizing hormone remedy pleasant after you have had a communicate of the dangers and blessings similarly to remedy options with a fitness care company who has knowledge in transgender care. Make sure you understand what will seem and get answers to any questions you could have before you begin hormone remedy.

Feminizing hormone remedy generally starts with the useful resource of taking the medicine spironolactone (Aldactone). It blocks male sex hormone receptors — additionally referred to as androgen receptors. This lowers the amount of testosterone the body makes.

About 4 to 8 weeks while you begin taking spironolactone, you begin taking estrogen. This moreover lowers the amount of testosterone the body makes. And it triggers physical modifications inside the frame which might be due to girl hormones inside the route of puberty.

Estrogen may be taken severa approaches. They encompass a pill and a shot. There also are several forms of estrogen which might be executed to the pores and skin, which include a cream, gel, spray and patch.

It is extraordinary no longer to take estrogen as a tablet when you have a non-public or family records of blood clots in a deep vein or inside the lungs, a circumstance referred to as venous thrombosis.

Every different preference for feminizing hormone remedy is to take gonadotropin-liberating hormone (Gn-RH) analogs. They decrease the amount of testosterone your frame makes and may can help you take decrease doses of estrogen with out the use of spironolactone. The downside is that Gn-RH analogs generally are greater high-priced.

While you start feminizing hormone remedy, you may be aware the subsequent adjustments to your frame over time:

Fewer erections and a decrease in ejaculation. This could begin 1 to three months after remedy starts offevolved. The overall impact will happen inside 3 to 6 months.

Tons less hobby in intercourse. This is also called decreased libido. It will begin 1 to 3 months once you start treatment. You may see the total effect within 1 to 2 years.

Slower scalp hair loss. This may begin 1 to a few months after treatment starts. The overall effect will appear interior 1 to 2 years.

Breast development. This starts 3 to six months after remedy starts. The whole effect takes region within 2 to three years.

Softer, much less oily pores and pores and skin. This could start 3 to six months after remedy begins offevolved. This is additionally when the complete impact will occur.

Smaller testicles. This also is known as testicular atrophy. It starts 3 to 6 months after the start of remedy. You could see the general impact within 2 to three years.

Much less muscle companies. This could begin three to six months after treatment starts offevolved. You may see the overall impact within 1 to 2 years.

More frame fat. This could start three to six months after treatment starts. The whole impact will appear inner 2 to 5 years.

Less facial and frame hair boom. This could begin 6 to twelve months after treatment starts offevolved. The entire impact takes place inside 3 years.

A number of the physical modifications due to feminizing hormone remedy may be reversed in case you save you taking it. Others, along with breast development, can't be reversed.

Consequences

Whilst on feminizing hormone remedy, you meet frequently together with your fitness care issuer to:

Maintain song of your physical modifications.

Show your hormone degrees. Over the years, your hormone dose can also need to change to ensure you take the bottom dose crucial to get the bodily outcomes which you need.

Have blood tests to test for changes on your ldl ldl cholesterol, blood sugar, blood rely, liver enzymes and electrolytes that might be due to hormone therapy.

Display your behavioral health.

You furthermore mght need habitual preventive care. Depending on your situation, this can include:

Breast maximum cancers screening. This must be carried out consistent with breast most cancers screening guidelines for cisgender women your age.

Prostate maximum cancers screening. This ought to be completed in line with prostate cancer screening suggestions for cisgender guys your age.

Monitoring bone fitness. You need to have bone density assessment in keeping with the suggestions for cisgender girls your age. You can need to take calcium and weight-reduction plan D nutritional supplements for bone fitness.

THE END